I0766737

Don't Join the Army YET!!

Don't Join the Army YET!!

Timmy Lynch

Copyright © 2020 by Timmy Lynch.

| ISBN: | Softcover | 978-1-7960-9483-1 |
| | eBook | 978-1-7960-9482-4 |

All rights reserved. No part of this book may be reproduced or transmitted in any form or by any means, electronic or mechanical, including photocopying, recording, or by any information storage and retrieval system, without permission in writing from the copyright owner.

Any people depicted in stock imagery provided by Getty Images are models, and such images are being used for illustrative purposes only. Certain stock imagery © Getty Images.

Print information available on the last page.

Rev. date: 03/18/2020

To order additional copies of this book, contact:
Xlibris
1-888-795-4274
www.Xlibris.com
Orders@Xlibris.com
706082

Contents

INTRODUCTION

THE PURPOSE OF this book is to help provide guidance to the 0.5 percent of the population that will join the military. With volunteers being the first-generation soldiers, sailors, and marines, most will have little or no knowledge of military life. This book outlines a basic plan that will allow you to have an idea before you join the military or even apply for your first job if its right for you.

Labor is the first measure of value.
–Adam Smith

CHAPTER 1

Recruited

THERE WAS NO school that day. My brothers and I were headed to the Texas State Fair, so I counted my money and separated my bus fare from the few dollars I had saved up; it was not much, but I could still have a great time. After two transfers and twenty minutes of standing on the bus, we arrived. Walking toward the entrance, a sea of people were flowing in and out the gates, some eating food, others carrying prizes of all sizes. I handed the attendant my pass; we were all in, time to put our plan into action. First stop was the roller coaster. Big wooden and scary looking, I was strapped in; it crept to a slow start up the hill. The first car reached the top. I held on tight. For the next few minutes twist and turns praying that the ride would finally end, it came to a screeching halt; exiting the ride, I walked as if I'd just conquered the beast instead of showing how just seconds ago I was just crouched in the fetal position. Good ride, now that my heart was racing. It was on to the scary house and house of mirrors. With some courage still intact, I tried my hand at winning a prize. After wasting a dollar or two trying to throw dimes into a bottle, we headed to the food stands, foot-long hotdogs covered with chili and cheese, freshly dipped corndogs, cotton candy, funnel cakes, and the must-have candied apples. We topped everything off with a bag of popcorn for the road. The next stop was hours of walking to every exhibit and museum, the only time of year where we could visit everything for free–giant mammoth bones, dinosaurs and stuffed bears, beautiful plants and fish, artwork under armed guard, bust of people some you've never heard of, portraits of George Washington and the Founding Fathers, science exhibits of items that would now be common place, and microwave oven and color television.

Now the highlight of the day, the long-awaited car shows, this was not just walking around dreaming of owning that Mustang or Corvette. No, that was for rookies. We had to go straight to the free giveaways. We would get our free bag so we could grab every free pen and brochure.

After signing up for every free window estimate and spa treatment, I stopped by what seemed like a recruiting station for every branch of the military. Well, after listening to what would nowadays be considered a pitchman, I filled out information cards so I could get that fancy-looking pen or pencil, or if they were really trying, a T-shirt. Walking away with the goods, I felt pretty good because I had no intentions of ever joining. Little did I know, that for the next few weeks I would be harassed for my greed. At 9:00 p.m., it was time to head home, bags filled and money gone and another great year at the fair.

It was time to pay for my greed, as each recruiter did their follow-up calls. As my senior year was drawing near, the thought of joining, well it didn't sound so bad, but what would I choose after seriously listening to each recruiter again. I had to go by what I'd heard and what the recruiter was saying. The air force recruiter made me feel like an idiot. The navy, the thought of being out at sea for months, no way, I'd never been away from home more than a few weeks, and that was to visit my grandparents. The marines, I had spoken with an ex-marine, telling him I was considering on joining. He scared me so bad I didn't think I could ever measure up to become one. I left, believing that old saying that marines were brainwashed. I later realized that they had a much-higher standard than I was willing to give. Well, finally the army, just like the story of the three bears—this soup was too hot; this one was too cold. The army was just right. One may ask why, but for some they were inspired by the movies like *Rambo* or the multitude of army movies like *The Green Berets* or *Tora! Tora! Tora!* or just continuing a tradition of family service. For me, it was the idea of having a skill and regular pay. Now having made up my mind, the real test was to sell the idea to my mother. Prior to my school year ending, I had two brothers that decided that I had a good idea and quickly joined, so mom wasn't too pleased with having three sons in the military, but like with my brothers, this would be my only way out if I wanted a better future. Besides I still had year to change my mind. Having gotten past these two hurdles, the recruiter had to see if I were even smart enough to even join because for me school was just some place I had to go and stay out of trouble. I really hated being there. I felt like the service would teach me a skill that I would really use. Besides no one used history or algebra, right! After scheduling and taking my entrance test, I scored high enough to join. I would at this point be placed in the Delayed Entry Program (DEP). Today it's called the Future Soldiers Program; this is a program where individuals going into active duty in the United States Armed Forces enlist first in the DEP before they ship out to basic training or boot camp.

CHAPTER 2

Four Years Hard Labor

AFTER A TEARFUL goodbye, on that Friday morning, I was headed to the military entrance processing station in Dallas, Texas, not to be seen again by some for four years. From this point on my life would have several of **my firsts**–my first plane ride, **my first** trip to another state, and later **my first** trip out of the country. After swearing in and multiple pokes and prods, I boarded a plane headed to the reception station, Fort Jackson, South Carolina with my brand-new army-issued haircut and a duffel bag of gear. We were loaded on to what was once called a cattle car, today a Troop Carrier, where I would meet several men that would change my life, and the way I would see it forever, for nine weeks I would love and hate these men. And like my own father, maybe even more so, I would do all I could to never let them down; they were the closest thing to a real superhero I ever met. At the end of those nine weeks, I knew I had made the right decision. Fort Gordon, Georgia, here I would be taught the skills that would fulfill my contract, two months here and then off to my new home for the next eighteen months, Fort Bragg, North Carolina. At this place, I would meet some of the greatest and worst soldiers, one could ever meet.

Being home of the airborne and Delta Force, the atmosphere was truly thick with pride. If one were infantry, one had better be airborne. If not, one would be a dirty leg. A leg is an infantry soldier that walked everywhere he went. This was considered to be the lowest of the low. The next level was mechanized infantry, soldiers that rolled into war in iron chariots. Finally the airborne, better known as death-from-above soldiers, if one jumped out of what we would consider a perfectly good aircraft. Even where you were in the platoon could be considered an insult. Troops in the first platoon thought of themselves as being the best and were second to none. Third platoon was the third herd, tough and rowdy. Now if one had a roommate from the Vietnam era one could be sharing a room with the biggest alcoholic and drug addict in the company. Those were the days before drug testing and PTSD, being a real diagnosis.

Fort Bragg had its mixture of realities. I was housed next to a building for six months before I realized it wasn't vacant; it had the company sign out front. It was a Special Forces Unit, but I never saw movement inside or a light on. I happened to one day see a soldier taking trash to the dumpster. Other than that, there was no more movement. Now this was the early eighties, well before cell phones and internet or twenty-four-hour news. It was that time when if you heard the name Delta Force, Special Forces, or Navy SEALs, it brought images of secret organization within the military, where you had to be superhuman to join and bred to be a killer the day you were born. Today you can research from your couch the requirements to be a mechanic to Army Ranger. My next set of orders sent me to Wharton Barracks, Heilbronn, Germany. Just when I thought I'd experienced the world, "Hello, beautiful mountains, dense forest, the autobahn, jaeger schnitzels, and the red light district." There I would truly understand the meaning of culture shock, being home sick and feeling loneliness. Germany would teach me more about myself than I would've liked to have known. In America hooters used to be considered sleazy; it doesn't come close to a German bar. In America, a sports bar is a nice place to watch sports and eat wings, maybe take the spouse. In Germany, one might not tell the wife were he was last night. If she found out he was in the red light district, he may end up in the divorce court the next day. "Why?" one could ask. Where can a man go have a meal and liquor, watch porn, and go upstairs and pick from some of the most beautiful women, and it's all perfectly legal. It can be a little overwhelming for someone who has spent most of his life in church, but in the end I found it hard to leave. There was something open and honest the way they treated life. Even the television programs were somehow pure at its core; there was nothing surprising to see a man walking around naked or a pair of breasts flash across the screen. Life in Germany made me question everything I had been taught; it was a life-changing experience, and I found it hard to leave behind.

CHAPTER 3

Motivated

$\mathbf{B}$ACK HOME, ANOTHER culture shock, how was that possible? Eighteen months in another state, twenty-four in another country, how do I return to normal and what was normal? Home felt like a foreign country. Old friends and family felt like strangers. They seemed like lazy and selfish people. My army family were people who ate cold food, slept two or three hours, and could go out on another mission that would have them out until the next morning. I trusted them with my life. Back home, I found it hard to even trust my own family members, but I had no time for self-pity; time to find work. Here was where being motivated came in. I set out with my new military skills just to find out that I was in the midst of a communications change. My expert knowledge of twenty-four-pair cable and switchboard operator was so antiquated; the only place that still used them was in the army. This turned out to be the discovery of the hidden anger I had inside, but not to worry, I was a warrior. I resorted to the one thing I used well and that was using my back. The next few days I would apply for general labor work. Within days I was working in a department store dock unloading trucks. The good and bad news were I could find plenty of minimum-wage work. My second bout with my hidden anger, I realized that I had to return to the one thing I hated and that was school, but try I would, I spent the next few years in and out of one college to the next. The problem was that I couldn't make the effort consistent, a semester here and there and never the same major. One year I was studying economics, the next criminal justice, and finally general science, never getting anywhere close to finishing. After several years out of the service and job hopping from dock to dock, I met an older gentleman who gave me some advice. The only problem with advice was that if one were not ready to accept it, it was worthless, but what he said I'd all ways remember. He said, "Get in a yard and stay there." I could keep jumping from one job to the next and one school to the next, but if I didn't change my thinking, I would stay in the same spot, so until I did that, the mop I was pushing would still be there, ready for me to push it no matter where I worked. He reminded me of the definition of the word insanity, doing the same thing and expecting a different result. So I took part of his advice. I found a job at a law firm, where I worked for the next five years, but still dropping in and out of colleges, I later learned that the traditional college classroom was just not for me. This lesson was learned after I read a book about education and how the school system used testing to determine your intelligence and not how well a teacher understood my teaching needs. After again making a job change, I found myself working the nightshift at a bus station; there I met a National Guard recruiter. Here I go again being recruited. So after answering a few questions, almost the same ones seven years earlier, I told him I only wanted to do one thing in the army and that was to fire weapons. He assured me that he had the right job for me. He asked me if I would be interested in firing mortars. Not knowing what a mortar was, I said yes. As in the years gone past, I was in a MEPS swearing in, still not knowing or even caring about what a mortar was. I was just happy to be back in, part of something I was familiar with the army. I would spend the next six years as an infantryman, learning and firing everything from the classic 1911 .45 caliber pistol to the smooth-bore 120 mm mortar, and to the newly assigned Bradley Fighting Vehicle, but learn I did. Not only how to properly engage the weapon, but how it felt when a mortar round got stuck in the tube. It put a new spin on how it felt to be close to death and an appreciation for the true deadly fire power of a Bradley, but as my six years with the guard ended, something was still missing. While I felt proud of being an infantryman, I blamed the army for not giving me a skill I could use as a civilian. So one day I looked up the word skill, which according to *Webster's* simply means "the ability to do something well." And just like that, by reeducating myself to the meaning of that one word, a great burden began to lift off my shoulders but was soon replaced by another word, frustration. Why! It was because my excuse of not having a skill was false and had been false for many years, but at that moment, I realized what I was and had always been, a professional soldier. I had been given the skills. People spend years and thousands of dollars to learn leadership, problem solving, and counseling skills. What I hadn't learned was how to apply those skills in my everyday life, and that those weren't just soldier skills; they were life skills. As I looked to continue my life as a part-time soldier, I looked into other areas to broaden my skills. I began researching the skills needed for an army recruiter. I didn't think I had salesmanship. This required me to be able to cold call and approach strangers—an army medic not a fan of needles, drill sergeant, again like the three bears. Just right, the ability to lead and teach others, so it was goodbye National Guard, hello Army Reserve. Here I would sign up for another six years. I spent the first six months learning again more about myself and others and how to use **POWER**. There were those who respect it and those who abuse it, and the line between them was very thin. Long before hazing on college campuses became spotlighted on headline news, the military was the poster boy for hazing. While this was a way to weed out those not loyal to your group, there were those who use cruel tactics as a way of getting revenge on new members, for the brutality done to them in the name of camaraderie, but early in my training, I knew and understood the purpose of a drill sergeant and held the position highly. Applying what I learned, of all the knowledge I gained at the academy, the most valuable one was *learning styles*. I found out my best learning environment wasn't sitting eight hours in a classroom reading a book or even working math problems on a chalkboard or someone demonstrating how an engine worked, my style was a combination of all three. Once I learned this, I immediately understood my dislike for school, and why I spent so much time in and out of college, it was just a continuation of the twelve years of public school. "Okay, class, read chapters 1–5 and then write a three-page essay, in your own words on why Columbus discovered America, single spaced."

I would immediately get right on that once I left the basketball court. Thank God for summer breaks, a used lawn mower, .75 cents a gallon of gas, paper routes, and summer work programs. These things along with an encouraging mother kept me out of trouble. But knowing my learning style wasn't enough to completely change my life, it also took motivation, which was the one thing the academy made sure we possessed before we graduated. Returning home from the academy, I felt as if I had a veil removed from my eyes. I not only saw the many flaws in my life but the negative and unmotivated behavior in others. We were all floating through life doing the same things and expecting a different outcome, the true definition of insanity. So I began to research how did this begin.

CHAPTER 4

The Education System

SO WHERE DID it begin? With the arrival of the *Mayflower*, it not only brought with it indenture servitude, it also brought those fleeing religious persecution and also an education system. In 1647, the general court of Massachusetts Bay Colony decreed that every town that reached a certain population shall have an elementary and Latin school; this was to ensure that all Puritan children learn to read the Bible and receive basic information about their Calvinist religion. In 1779 one of the Founding Fathers Thomas Jefferson purposed a two-track educational system, consisting of the laboring and the learned, providing very few scholarships to the laboring class and limiting their chances for advancement. It was what Jefferson quoted, "By raking a few geniuses from the rubbish." By 1827 Massachusetts passed a law making all grades of public school open to all pupils free of charge. By 1830 most Southern states had established laws forbidding to teach people in slavery to read. Today's education is free to all, with a budget of

$620 billion (public and private). But according to a recent study, there are still 32 million adults in the US that can't read, with 21 percent reading below a fifth-grade level. While this information answered some questions, it didn't answer the one question I had and that was where was I going? This turned out to be the most important question to answer because it created more questions, like what did I want to be and how do I get there, and just as important, where do I start? As I joggled with these questions, it became clear that if I answered the question of what do I want to be, it answered where was I going because it provided some direction, but like every kid who was ever asked this question, one might as well stand back and watch his head explode, trying to figure that out.

One would be better off asking a toddler, "What does $E = mc^2$ mean?" Most adults can't answer that question. The answer is E is energy, m is mass, and c is speed of light. So energy equals the amount of mass times the speed of light squared. Okay, so what does this have to do with what do I want to be? Well, depending upon how much energy I put into mass, my brain, this may determine how fast I reach my destination. It's simple, right? So I began to make a list of things I thought I wanted to be. As I wrote this list, I stopped because you see I realized that other factors and questions popped up, the fact that I wasn't a teenager planning his life. I was thirty-eight years old, and the question of what I wanted to be and where I was going had more significance because time had now become a factor. I had less of it, so I decided to address this from a personal issue at a later date. So I posed this question to my son. As I expected he had no idea, so we began to work on an answer together. To help us get started, I posed another question, which was what kind of lifestyle did he want, meaning did he want to someday drive an expensive car and what kind, and what was his idea of an expensive car, what kind of house, did he someday want kids? If so, did he want to prepare for their future, again meaning did he want to setup a college plan for them, and if so what kind of school did he want them to be able to choose from, a two-year community college or four-year university with housing off campus? I know these were hard questions to ask a teenager, but I explained to him that he could just float through life and hope good things happen to him or he could plan his success, so with this in mind, we started to answer the little questions first. Like when he decided to leave home to be on his own, did he want to own a car or ride public transportation? He answered, "Own a car" with pride.

So I then asked, "New or used, a Ford or Chevy, a Mustang or Corvette, are you going to pay cash or get a loan, what's your credit score, how do you plan to start a credit history?" Having more questions than answers, I could see his frustration developing, so I assured him that I would help him to paint a picture, one with color and form that he understood because he would paint it. I placed all the questions in a hat. We then began to answer them one by one. The first question was credit score. I explained that this question was simple to answer and resolve but required consistent attention and commitment. One way was to get a secured credit card meaning, one that he funded himself. Most secured cards usually required a $300 deposit, he could then make small purchases, pay them off in full every month. For several months, this would give him a credit history. The sooner he could start and maintain a good history, the better his score. The next question about buying a car, I explained this type of issue would require him to have a team, but not all of the members actually worked together and may only have one or two people in it. This team consisted of a loan officer or company. The better ones were credit unions, a mechanic, and the credit score if it had a good rating when he was ready to start looking or his own money if he planned to pay cash. Loan officers, these were the persons (financial institute) that would provide him the loan while giving him a good rate hopefully, based on your credit score. A mechanic, if one was not mechanically inclined, this was a good person to have to help with the purchase. He could look over the car to give a second opinion as to the condition of the vehicle. He was only needed if one was buying a used car. The worst thing one would want to do was to make payments on a broken car or truck. Once one decided on the vehicle, now began the science or goal of the purchase. That was to come as close to paying what the vehicle was worth, meaning if the car or truck was worth according to all the resources that would track and appraise vehicles. One would want to pay at or below market value. For example, if the vehicle was appraised at $10,000, one's goal was to get that vehicle for $10,000, including the interest on the loan, so if the vehicle was for sale for $10,000 and the loan was $10,000 with an interest rate of 5 percent, the total loan would be $10,500. That meant one would pay $500 more than the car is worth. One would need to decide if it was worth paying $500 more than the market value, which was a personal decision.

On my own or not, that was the question.

What does being on your own really mean? it means paying your own rent, and that's if you can prove you earn enough to afford the monthly payment. Then there's the ability to eat and shower. Back at your parents' house, you flip the light switch and they came on, go to the fridge and sure enough mom's got your favorite ice cream. Before, you never gave this a second thought, but now if you move two blocks in the wrong direction, it could mean coming home to an empty apartment, or two blocks uptown could mean luxury apartments with all the amenities you ever wanted, but you're eating ramen noodles with sliced wieners and hot sauce every night. For some college students that was a gourmet meal. Being on your own can be a very trying time. When you're on your own you can quickly find out what it's like to have to choice between the brand of soap you've used for years or some store brand that irritated your skin and how easily it is to justify the fact that you're not cheap, you're fugal. And all of a sudden you discover that they have been hiding coupons at the entrance of the grocery store and in your mail box, and if you use that buy-one-get-one-free burger coupon, you can eat for two days. After living this type of lifestyle for a while, you earn your black belt in frugality. Like a shaolin monk, you enter the thirty-three chambers of thriftiness. The day that you are allowed to leave, you are armed with the wisdom of why your mother yelled at you to close the refrigerator door or why your dad walked around like a sentry turning off lights in rooms with no one in them or how you learn how to make the best sandwich with the end pieces of a loaf of bread instead of tossing them out. But you must also beware of all of those early-morning infomercial, the ones you never gave a second glance now hold the secret to all of your financial woes, and if you believe for just $29.99, then just follow these ten steps and another $2,000 dollars later, you too can be rich. The real lesson you learned is the one who got rich wasn't you. It's that guy who was laid off and spent his last $30 dollars to purchase the program and behold six months later, he lives in a $2 million-dollar house in Florida. You know the one—Richard M or Sara T of Georgia, people you have never heard of. They are so rich that they are afraid to give you their full name, and the truth is while some of these programs may work, the fact is if you woke up tomorrow and your neighbor's house is for sale for $500 bucks, you still can't afford it. It doesn't matter if it's a million-dollar opportunity, that "knocking the idea is to learn how to put yourself in a position to take advantage of it." So that would leave the question, how do you do it? Well, it should have started at home.

The problem with being human is that from the moment we are born, we rely on our mother for survival and later our father, but there are no rules that say we have to know what we're doing to be a parent.

If we were to compare humans to any other species on the planet, the human female can become fertile as early as twelve years old. For any other species, that can be a very mature or even be considered an old animal. For humans we don't want our kids to even think about sex, let alone actually give birth, but we are the only species that will send our young into the world unable to provide for themselves. The moment a deer gives birth, the fawn knows that it must be up and running within minutes or it will be killed. As soon as a bee chews its way free from its cocoon, it is ready to begin working. Humans will provide food and shelter for eighteen years but may never provide one lesson on how to survive on its own. The short answer could be that we can't teach what we don't know.

As my son and I started the list, he gave me the usual answer of wanting to be an athlete, so I told him instead of giving me a long list, we would take a job one at a time and use one of our greatest resources, the internet. So we typed professional athlete and researched it. We both discovered that only 3 percent of high school athlete play at college level, and only 1 percent of them will go pro. We then researched doctors and found out that there was 1 doctor for every 300 people. I then explained to him that it wasn't important for us to just make a list, but it had to be achievable and meet the requirements for the lifestyle he wanted. He said that he didn't just want to work for someone but to one day own his own business, so again we did the research this time. We chose optometrist as a career. The educational requirement was a four-year degree.

The average startup cost for an optometrist are the following:

Office building cost / furniture–$13,000
Computer / office supplies–$3,000
Display cases for frames–$7,000
Initial advertisement / marketing–$2,000
Cost of frames to start–$10,000
Cost of contact lenses–$3,000
One time cost of $35,000
Leasing a medium-sized office–$35,00/month
Eye exam equipment cost–$1,500
Payroll (only one staff member) $1,600/month for only 4 days
Payroll tax for one employee–$400/month
Business insurance–$150/month
Phone / internet–$300/month

Electricity / Heat–$800/month
Accountant's fee–$300/month
New inventory investment–$800/month
Advertisement–$300
Other general monthly expenses–$500
Cost for the clinic to run–$10,000/month
1000 x 4 = $4,000 + $35,000 = $75,000 for 4 months

The office would be open four days week. So after this lesson on picking his lifestyle and career to help him reach that goal, I explained to him what he faced if he didn't choose his path and left it to chance.

In 2016 the poverty line for a single person is $11,880, a family of four is $24,300, and the minimum wage for 2016 is $7.25 per hour or $13,390 per year. To put this into perspective, the average rent in the US is $450 or $5,400 per year, electricity bill is $50 per month or $600 per year, add another $50 or $600 per year for water and sewer. There could also be an additional $50 or $600 a year for gas. Just working for minimum wage this leaves you with $6,790 at the end of a work year, which is not bad. If you don't plan on eating and you walk to work, the average car insurance for an 18-year-old is $3000 or $250 a month. As of 2015 the average price of a used car is $15,000, not including interest or $417 a month or $5,000 per year. For a total $8,000 from the $6,790 you have left, and you still haven't eaten a bite, but you are already in the red or negative $1,210. Now all of the information provided is based on the minimum wage of $7.25 per hour. So you may be asking what's the point? Well, unless you are one of the fortunate few whose parents have planned and prepared for your future and attended at least a decent school, you may find yourself one of the 1.2 million high school dropouts, which is a student every second or 7,000 a day, which leads to an uneducated, unskilled worker who will find it very difficult to find any kind of work that pays more than the minimum wage.

CHAPTER 5

Predicament

AS WE CONTINUED researching together, now came the truth,. My son now feeling a little picked on, fired back, "WELL, DAD! Did you prepare for my future?"

With my heart in my throat, 'cause I wasn't ready for that one, I said yes and no. No, I didn't have a savings for college, but yes, I had my benefits for twenty years of service. I could transfer it to him. Was the problem solved? It was not even close. While I earned the benefits for me, I owed him the opportunity to progress. So as I explained to him my predicament, we worked together on how I could pay for his education as well as my own. We agreed that I would set aside enough of my benefits to pay for one year of college and that we would make further decision on his education after. Feeling better about his and my future, we returned to our researching. I asked him a general question, "What is being rich? Google defines rich as a net worth of 2.3 million dollars." We also researched poor and middle class. After we put all the research together, the information was so varied that we left it to our own definition.

His was to be able to work enough to cover his expenses and do a little traveling. I agreed with his definition on the surface. I told him I was working to achieve the same, but with passive income, my money was working for me. Hearing this he became angry, stating that everything we discussed was for nothing. I reassured him that what we talked about was all relevant and that I was going to let him paint the picture.

CHAPTER 6

Planning

ANOTHER SKILL I was taught was how to plan and the importance of planning. Once I left the academy and was able to focus on my life, it would prove to be the most life-altering moment for me. It was the greatest awakening for anyone to know that they have direction and that each given moment served a purpose and not that every morning when we wake up we can only hope everything would work out.

It would be like a scene from an old black-and-white movie where some old uncle leaves you his entire estate worth millions, or some parent dies and up in the attic is an old trunk of your father's with a stack of stocks and bond now worth a fortune, not until you've learned the importance of planning do you even realize that as far-fetched as those movies seemed the results were from someone who planned ahead. Who they left their wealth to wasn't as important as to how they achieved it, so why was planning important? If you asked the average person where would they be in twenty years, an eighteen-year-old would probably say dead because they see the concept of being thirty-eight as being old. Others may say owning their own business, yet they don't know how to start a business or even have plans to attend business school. Now we may ask ourselves, why do I need to know this, why do I need to know where I'll be in twenty years, ten years or even six months from now? Then the question I have is how many flights do you think leave out of a major airport? There are hundreds, thousands, every day, and do you think that these planes are just taking off and landing wherever they please or is there a plan? How would you know when to be at the airport, and how would you know where the plane was going? When I asked myself this question, I didn't have an answer either, and at that point I was already thirty-eight. Like most people I had put up my sails and was going wherever life took me, but the problem was I appeared to be headed nowhere, and like a eighteen-year-olds, I still couldn't answer what I wanted to be. So having the skills of developing a plan was useless, and at that point I realized that life had made a plan for me. And it was to work me until I died because I hadn't developed a plan to live, so what does that mean? A plan to live, I never knew what kind of job I wanted, what kind of house, car, neighborhood to raise my kids, a wife, how many kids. Since I had no answer for these questions, life answered them for me. I didn't know what kind of lifestyle I wanted. I was left with a lifestyle of poverty for most of my life. It wasn't until I developed a plan that my life began to change.

So how do you develop a plan? First, let's understand the types of plans. There are two types that I use, and they are forward and reverse planning. Forward planning, that is to start from wherever you are and then plan forward to where you want to be. An example could be today I work as a cashier at a convenience store, but I want to someday be a manager, so I develop a plan to get the skills needed to qualify as a manager, whether that means getting into the management program at work if they offer it or taking an online course to receive a certificate or finally, if it means returning to school to get a degree, but whichever step you take, set time lines along the way until you reach your goal. Reverse planning works a little differently; it starts with your end state then you work backward, but because some goals require time to complete, you must make sure you include time as a factor. If you are required to have a bachelor's degree and you don't have any college degree, you must factor in at least three and a half to four years into your plan, so in a five-year plan, you must start in year one to reach your goal by year four to meet the requirements of year five. There are a lot of plans—long term, short term, tactical, or strategic. The key is to understand and develop a plan and follow it, and most importantly, your plan must be flexible or as they say fluid, being able to adjust your plan is a must. You will find that if you believe in and follow your plan, the level of stress and anxiety will be nominal.

CHAPTER 7

Unhappy Still

OKAY, NOW LET'S fast forward. You've put in the time, and you've made all the sacrifices to reach your goal just to realize, you didn't make the most important plan of all, your life's plan.

I'm working as a manager, I have the degrees, I have the debt to prove it, and I'm still not satisfied. Why? It's because like a big block of Swiss cheese, my plan has a bunch of holes in it. Yes, I made a plan to earn a living, but I didn't choose a career, one that fulfilled all of my dreams; it's just a job.

Did you say to yourself, "I want to own my own business or run a nonprofit"? Was your plan too short, do you have the wrong plan or is it simply incomplete, did you achieve your goal then realized that the salary you are earning barely covers your rent, car, and a few other bills, and did you find through your journey the man or woman of your dreams and then discovered that 30,000 dollars a year is comfortable for a single person with a used car? But for a person with a partner that wants more out of life like kids and a dog, you must go back to the drawing board because you realize now that you need to earn three times as must to live the lifestyle you dreamed of, so you must reevaluate your life. If you are a small-town boy or girl at heart, dreaming of a small farm with chickens and pigs and a small organic garden, will your hometown with a population of 500 provide you the income to earn 30,000 or even 10,000? Okay, so I went through all this effort to explain planning just to learn that my plan failed, so why bother? Well, even generals understand that the best-made plans fail. The purpose of this book isn't to help you develop the perfect plan but to help you understand that success is not an accident. Successful people aren't necessarily smarter than you, stronger or faster, but what they do possess is a plan that put them in a position to achieve success. The point of *Don't Join the Army Yet!* isn't anti-army or anti-military. The purpose of this book is for the reader to learn through my mistakes and how to avoid them, also to understand that even if my parents had left me a college fund or even millions of dollars, without proper education, without proper guidance, it can all be lost. Again does that mean it won't be lost? No, no plan is perfect. Do not get caught up on the perfect plan. But how will your plan work, are you meeting time lines, are you making necessary adjustments when needed? One important factor to remember is why are you doing something, meaning why are you joining the army? Am I here for twenty years or four? If I'm here for twenty, what should I expect in year 2040? One example is I should at least achieve the rank of sergeant major for enlisting or lieutenant colonel as an officer. My home should be paid for as well as having several hundred thousand in savings, and live off on my retirement.

Now is this reality? Yes, what can or cannot be reality is the discipline it will take to stick to a plan for twenty years. I'll restate by not focusing on the plan but on how well you can keep to it. A plan as short as a few months can be a challenge. What you must understand is as soon as you develop a plan, the laws of nature will begin to try to destroy it. Let's think about a simple task, going to dinner with a friend next Friday. As uneventful as this task should be, by not planning, nature will make plans for you. That indicator on your dash you ignored for weeks turned out to be a warning that your alternator was bad, and it decided to quit that day. You didn't call your friend and made plans for Friday. Your friend decided to work overtime. Or something as simple as not checking the calendar and there's a major event that weekend, as a result seating takes an hour or longer. Now does having a plan mean things will go smoothly? No, but by planning, you can be better prepared to make adjustments.

CONCLUSION

THE PURPOSE OF *Don't Join the Army Yet* is not to help you decide to join the military or not but to help you understand if joining makes sense. Whether you are joining to continue a family tradition or for college money, it must make sense. One thing is true if you join, no one has to put up with all you'll go through but you. So joining for someone else is just not worth it. Join the army for the benefits; it makes a lot more sense than joining just to be a part of something bigger than yourself. The army has been and can be the springboard to a greater career, greater prosperity. It can lay the foundation for a secure future. Finally, if you don't have a reason to join, if for no other reason than to preserve the constitution, then don't.

www.ingramcontent.com/pod-product-compliance
Lightning Source LLC
Chambersburg PA
CBHW051424250726
48655CB00003B/1223